*heart*lands

# *heart*lands

Words and Images from the River Hull Corridor

with an introduction by
**John Osborne**

Photography by **Martin Peters**

Edited by **Shane Rhodes**

Published by the City Arts Unit of Kingston upon Hull City Council

**Hull History Centre**
www.hullhistorycentre org uk

First published 1998 by
The City Arts Unit , Kingston upon Hull City Libraries
Central Library, Albion Street,
Kingston upon Hull, HU1 3TF

ISBN 0 9501233 9 0

The publisher acknowledges the financial assistance of
Yorkshire & Humberside Arts and Hull CityVision Ltd.

CITYVISION

The publisher further acknowledges sponsorship from
J.R. Rix & Sons Ltd, Hull
Edwin Snowden & Co. Ltd, Hull

Designed by Anonymous Design 01482 871246
Printed by Oriel Printing Company

# CONTENTS

# Introduction

## City of Words

Philip Larkin's poem 'Here' neatly encapsulates the Janus-faced character of Hull and that isolated wedge of England over which it presides, the Plain of Holderness. For Hull is both a Here that is Anywhere and is Everywhere and, at the same time, a Here that is as individual and as pungent as a whiff of the fish-dock. The very place-name is dualistic, the majestic and resonant Kingston upon Hull being commonly abbreviated to plain dull Hull. This ambivalence between the nondescript and the romantic, the bleak and the unique, the humdrum and the exotic, has fascinated and compelled several generations of poets, novelists, dramatists and visual artists. This book is the latest testament to that continuing fascination.

There is, of course, a literal sense in which Hull is a Here that is Anywhere and Everywhere, for more than half of humanity presently resides in cities and by the year 2025 this is expected to rise to three-quarters. Most of these people do not dwell in glitzy metropolises like Barcelona, New York or Paris; but in smaller, less glamourous, more workaday cities like Hull, Detroit, Gdansk, Birmingham, Nagasaki or Pittsburg. Metaphorically speaking, most people in the world will shortly be living in Hull. It follows that any artist who can analyse and dissect the human condition as experienced in the Hull that is Here will simultaneously be speaking for and to a majority of the earth's inhabitants in all those Hulls that are Everywhere. This is the anonymous, representative Hull of commercial hustle, of the largest housing estate in Europe, of fierce sporting loyalties, of undistinguished architecture, of teenage pregnancy and drug addiction, and of lives of quiet desperation occasionally alleviated by appetency and resolution. It is the Hull of Larkin's 'Mr Bleaney', Douglas Dunn's *Terry Street* and John Godber's play *Bouncers* and *Up and Under*.

The other side of the city, altogether more mysterious and exalted, is that which pertains to its riverine and maritime character, its nearness to the North Sea and the Baltic, its intimacy with water. Built on the confluence of two rivers, the tiny Hull and the two-mile-wide Humber, the original city was further enclosed by a circlet of inter-connecting docks which virtually severed it from the mainland and gave it a provisional, offshore, island identity. This is the city of gulls, mudflats and bridges; the city that once went fishing, is still the third largest port in the country but which is now given over to container ships and yachting marinas. It is the city of welcome signs in foreign languages, of Slave and Whaling Museums, of Larkin's "ships up streets", and of names like Dagger Lane and The Land of Green Ginger. This is the city of the Heartlands project, the Hull which is Here and not Elsewhere.

This unique, maritime Hull subsequently spawned another in the residential quarter known as The Avenues whose long, straight, tree-lined streets are thronged with Victorian and Edwardian houses built for the captains of the fleet when the fishing industry was at its peak. To the east this precinct is bounded by Pearson Park, which sports an ornate gateway, a serpentine and a Victorian conservatory. The whole area has a *louche*, melancholy elegance with its statues and plaques, its waterless fountains and its mansions subdivided into flats. When the naturalist Helen Crowther surveyed the site in 1996 she was able to report a variety of fauna and flora greater than in the countryside, the butterfly species outnumbering those at Barton Nature Reserve, and the animals including deer, red squirrel, barn owl, pipistrelle bats and crested newts. This city as the seedy interface between the urban and the rural has held a special magic for poets like Philip Larkin, Douglas Dunn,

George Kendrick, Peter Didsbury and Sean O'Brien (two of whose books, *The Indoor Park* and *HMS Glasshouse*, are titled after the Victorian conservatory). Although a mile or two away from the nearest dock, The Avenues area is connected to it by Hull's flatness and closeness to the water-table; for in rainy weather paving-stones tip-tilt with a squelch, as though the city foundations were just inches thick, tarmac floated on water. This is Kingston upon Hull, the Venice of the North.

When the City Arts Unit commissioned the photographer Martin Peters to document the River Hull corridor, it might have been expected that only the more romantic side of the city would be memorialised. However, the photographs candidly choreograph the schizophrenic character of the place, wild skies and sun-struck waterways coinciding with a bricky male-dominated world of industrial chimneys, warehouses, mills and subterranean toilets; a half-hidden hermetic world of uniforms, tunics and rubber gloves; a factory landscape of Boilermakers, Tankworks and Electric Welders. This same juxtaposition of beauty and squalor, dilapidation and renewal, is there in the poems - some of them directly inspired by Peters' photos, all of them penned by writers with Hull links.

This brings us to a final Hull, the one the expatriate Australian writer Peter Porter described as the most poetical city in England. This is the city that at one time or another has played host to novelists like Dorothy L Sayers, Winifred Holtby, Malcolm Bradbury, Daphne Glazer and Heather Ingman; to dramatists like Alan Plater, John Godber and Anthony Minghella (now best known, of course, as the director of such movies as *Truly, Madly, Deeply* and *The English Patient*); of cultural commentators like Jacob Bronowski, Richard Hoggart and Jonathan Raban; and to poets who, in addition to those already mentioned, include golden oldies like Andrew Marvell and William Mason, and more modern practitioners like Stevie Smith, Brian Higgins, Frank Redpath, Ken Smith, Roger McGough, Tom Paulin, Douglas Houston, Andrew Motion, Tony Flynn, T.F.Griffin, Oliver Reynolds, Susan Wicks, Maggie Hannan and Christopher Greenhalgh - together, of course, with the mostly younger talents gathered in these pages. All of these writers, plus a plethora of painters, photographers and rock musicians, have taken this drably-enchanting Janus-faced city and transfigured it into art. Perhaps when the Hull of fishing and rugby has been all but erased by the merciless amnesia of time, the city will live on, like the New Orleans of jazz, in a thousand poems and pictures. In the last analysis, the most durable Hull, the one that is Now and Always, Here and Everywhere, may not be the one made of bricks and brine but this other Heartland, this City of Words.

John Osborne
Hull University
21 October, 1998

Ian Parks        FROM DRYPOOL BRIDGE

A rusting girder intersects
the partial view.  From here
you'll glimpse the city's
underside: a web of dreams,
a net of solitudes
that leads you on and out
past rotting wharf, still waterway -
a darkening centre
where no light intrudes.
Not now, but one day soon
the stilted city will decay,
the whole thing sinking
back into the sea.
Till then the place
exists between two tides.
The city floats on its own dream,
tilts to the source, subsides.

**Ian Parks**  THE OBERON

I spent a rainy afternoon
among the city's dissident;
drank tepid bitter
from a clouded glass
as the barmaid blinked
a tear back from her eye.
Outside, the world
of commerce came and went
in a far-off quarter
that survived the blitz.
My girl arrived
too early or too late.
It was a dream, a non-event
in which the city
realigned its course.
We stepped into
the bright, impartial day
in a city of lost chances
where the rail lines terminate.

Susan Wicks    FOUNTAIN ROAD, 1967/98

The photograph's bent gleam
holds our four plates
and not much more -
one of those winter afternoons
when darkness rose like smog
from the pavements.  You look half-cut
as you lean to fill my mug
with wine - older than you do now,
thirty years later... Fountain Road
through a brown fug
of fingerprints or steam,
and the three of us, heads bowed
as if to say grace.
I hardly know
which of those girls I was.

The house is gone, you tell me,
the street razed
and built again, our wishbones
ground to powder, half the place
grass.  Nothing I recognise
but sky; a newer house,
a table spread
with things to sell:
'Children playing.  Fountain Road.'
I need a magnifying glass
to make it out, the *Power Ranger*
written on a child's face.

Jules Smith        TOMORROW'S PEOPLE

could be figures in a Breughel landscape,
raking fields, bending with peasant postures
from ancestor lifetimes that worked the land,
and were cut-down, gathered, buried, burnt.
Or they could be tending their allotments,
these men in old sweaters and brown trousers,
made redundant years back, 'doing something',
parodying an agrarian past.

Gravestones say nothing.  Only the sky knows,
the sky agelessly blue, and crossed
with vapour trails; building, dispersing clouds,
the restless backdrop to a Make Work scheme.
This is a cemetery.  No daft place.
The place for those with nothing else to do.
Just the place for couples, to talk it through.
Where people talk to stones and look at space.

But there stands a young woman wearing black,
the Goddess of all cutbacks in this scheme
of things, holding Art's clippers in her hands,
ready to cut the threads of life, of work.
Her lips are Revlon-painted, dark cherry.
The whole scene is about to be f-stopped.
Yesterday's Men are Tomorrow's People.
One of them looks up.  The Goddess smiles.  Click.

Jules Smith     THE MANXMAN IN FOG

Minerva's owl keeps its watch on the gull,
close by the Fruit Trades and butchers of Hull,
near the old ferry, Victoria Pier.
Even shitehawks are offal eaters here.

The mating of sea-roke and Larkin's face
produced this odd, drably magical place,
where paper tides amid the sea of print
attract terminal types, most of them skint.

Thus, Hull Poets.  Eclectic in religion,
they're all Apollo's - or Sam Smith's - children,
who hailed the White Goddess with pub-lunch and pints,
becoming this sea-city's secular saints.

                              *

"Last Orders"; the best state to start the quest.
"Your waitress today is Mary Celeste".
Leviathan aural enchantments boom
soft fog-horn ways through the smoke-filled room.

Moist mist wears Venus slippers, Neptune's gown,
round a ghost ship tied up in the Old Town.
Fiction's Creatures on the S.S.'Manxman',
that disco-lights boat our Flying Dutchman.

Notionally bound for New Holland pier,
pursuing love and fame, faith and beer,
these scholars lived out their maritime dreams
of language, then wrote and pissed in streams.

They played down the mind-hold, an indoor park
for flora, fauna, strange fish in the dark.
They paid time's dollar, and found cures for youth,
on a vessel lacking only daylight truth...

*

Money's bustle, art's unconscious idyll;
to get them both on board, that's the riddle.
Now it's gone, strangled by debt, towed elsewhere;
the 'Brigadoon' boat's dry-docked in thin air.

Helen Dunmore        GIRAFFES IN HULL

Walking at all angles
to where the sky ends,
wantons with crane-yellow necks
and scarlet legs
stepping eastward, big eyes
supping the horizon.

Watch them as they go, the giraffes
breast-high to heaven,
herding the clouds.
Only Hull has enough sky for them.

Seamus Curran     CHILD'S PLAY

Sack bag-clothed
bin shield-fronted
stick-sworded
we set them pacing -

Romans or Slaves.
We chased them amongst ragweed
or were found under
a knot of tented grass-spears.

Then fleeing amongst graves
we hid between the chestnut
trunks and the wall, finding
there a ready-made death trail;

a late wake of wrought handles
and dulled crucifixes, like those
that weighted rosary beads,
only larger.  The rotted wood

of coffins gave way under our feet.
The stained linen clung to the inside
as staunch as ivy, surprising us
with its staying power

and by its reverent human touch.
Were these all death's treasures
then?  No skulls or rib cages,
only those soiled remnants?

This hoard of ornamental fittings
I hid under a sod at the back
of the field.  When touched
these anonymous relics that had been

ousted from graves, surrendered
not a glimmer of their mystery.
I bagged my little heap of death's credentials
and slung them over the graveyard wall.

Hiding amongst the chestnut trees
we would have raised spirits
with outstretched fingers
and be stunned to the marrow.

There we raved and crooned,
vampires and ghouls, trampling
the redundant trappings
into their final graves.

Peter Didsbury    FAR FROM THE HABITATIONS OF MEN

Multiple exposure,
the living and the dead.
Ghostly tanners
move silently round a hide.
Their spirit knives flash and flense,
as swift as thought, definitive as text.
Talmud forbids the former synagogue
to be put to this trade's uses.
Mayhew's dog-shit collector,
once a child,
was about these streets
till as late as 1950.

Peter Didsbury     HEARTLAND

*i.m. Frank Stansfield*

But whose heart,
since Hitler bombed
the Puseyites out of Sculcoates?
High Explosive, emptier of parishes,
'tumbled' from the bomb-bays.
What need was here of stones,
when sticks it seems
had been thus empowered against bone?
And yet must leave 'old Frank', even until last year,
bent almost double,
for single witness almost, almost even for saint.
Low and unadorned modernity
squats as sheltered housing across
the vanished streets whose names it dares to retain.
St Michael, All the Angels,
Augustine of Hippo, Monica his mother.
'Take and eat', calls a voice from a silent garden.
'To walk to work the way you are taking now
is to graze among death assemblages,
be nourished by the taphonomy of worship'.

Carol Coiffait       BOXING THE COMPASS

You can stay
in one place
only long enough
to find your way
to the chip-shop,
the bus-stop
and back home

Or longer:
To make a net
of seven
interlocking
streets, a leaping
stag from the old
tree at the corner
and to see stars
slide west
along the wires.

More than half
a life spent
in one place
and you're shunted
from the horizon
to the river-smell
into a taxi-cab, a bar
and back again
on one street name
a half-remembered face
a certain quality
of light or rain
past "I work here."
to "loved in vain.."
You ricochet
from then
to now
and back
in memory lane.

Carol Coiffait ROUGH HAVEN

Here, where they say the Romans crossed
The river is raw, a mangy dog
Chewing at its flank; great gobs of grass
And mud, slewing and shouldered
Field by sly field, off the northern bank.

All that is left for the beleaguered
Sheep and lambs, is one thin strip
Between a dousing and the trains.
This farmer's loss will be another's gain
As mud-flats shift and shift again.

Shane Rhodes        FOSSIL

Sometimes I just know
so I don't look.  Familiar streets
hold you, but I'm veiled.

Confucius reckons it's avoiding
the truth, and not going where
we might collect ideas

is keeping a cork in it.
Reasoning, well there is none,
and time is the anaesthetist;

it strips of all things white
then takes you to sludge,
leaving what's left on your bones

to do the rest.  I've learned
by rote the effigy of that dead
gull, with its twisted beaten

neck pressed into the boardwalk,
and how we left our bootleg footprints
somewhere round these parts.

I would have much preferred
them temporarily in sand
but we didn't have a sea;

only an old dock, a brown
corridor without a lid,
letting far too much light in.

Douglas Houston      ESSENTIALS

The sky fits the city perfectly.
High cranes and girdered bridges
Affirm in steel geometries
The open-handed rule agreed on
By the decks of barges,
The well-drained streets,
The full pint glasses,
Snooker tables, every well-set brick -
All in accord with the bottom line
Where light and air touch the planes of water,
Local, ubiquitous, wholly at ease with
its global monopoly on *horizontal.*

Following the annual discovery of summer
Reclining on a wardrobe full of sky
Held perfectly still in the river
Out behind some warehouses,
People lie in sunshine
With their eyes closed on lawns
Between buildings, on beds in houses
With all the windows open,
Smiling in pleasurable recognition
Of how well space fits their bodies,
The just simplicity of how things are,
Meetings, distinctions, the law of sky and water.

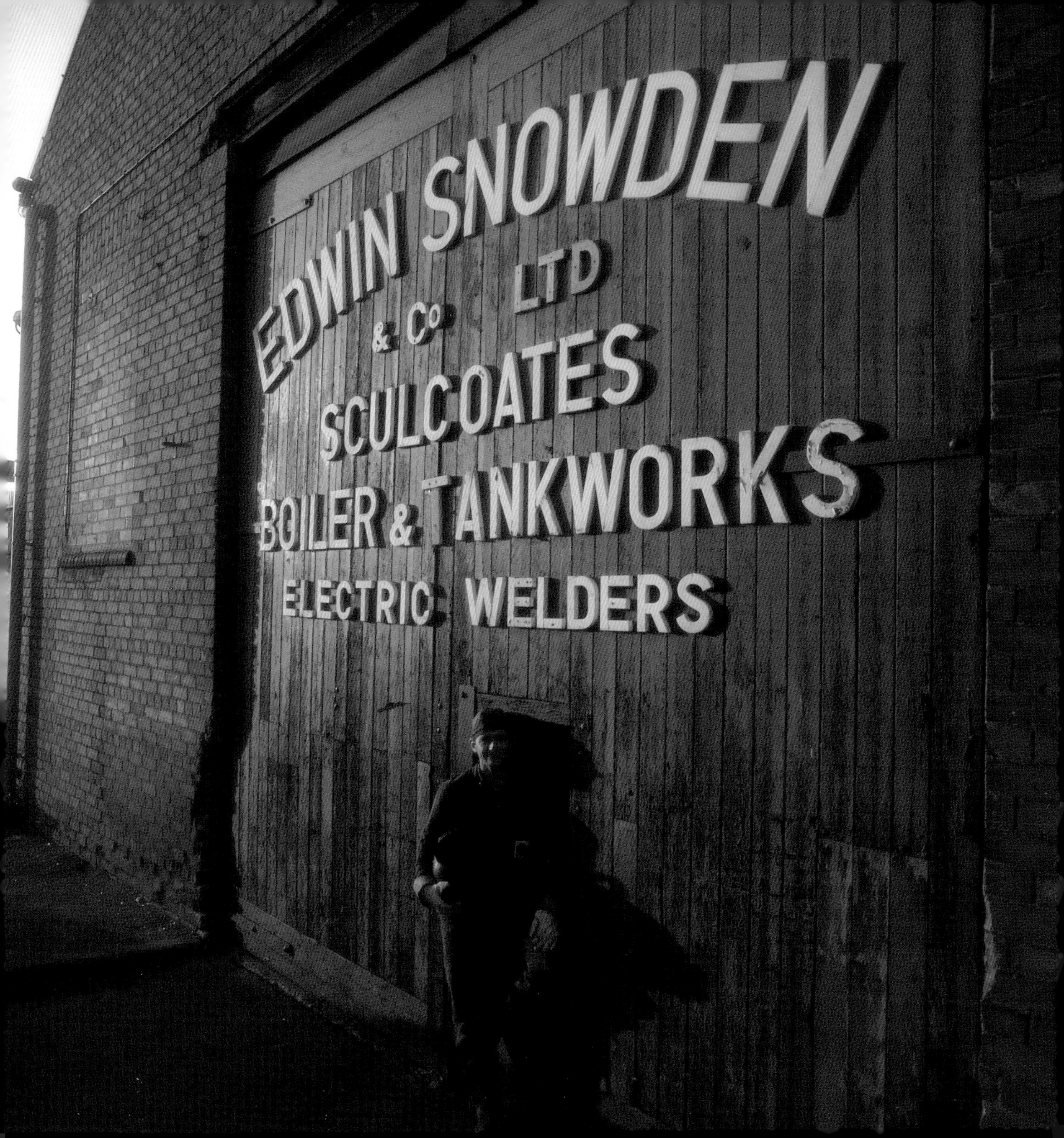
EDWIN SNOWDEN
& Co LTD
SCULCOATES
BOILER & TANKWORKS
ELECTRIC WELDERS

Dean Wilson     STRANGE MARKINGS

Don't like the sun rising
but I like it setting
'cos that's when I get an inkling
of what's in the offing

There's a place I go
but I don't know how I get there
and it feels like walking down Wincolmlee
breathing in the mucky air

you were the nearest thing
to redemption I will get
Alarm bells should have rang out loud
and maybe they did

but my head was too far
up in the clouds
and my feet everywhere
but on the ground

Haven't made my mark yet
which is just as well
'cos my blood's not my own
since you upped and left

and before too long
I'll get my just deserts
so I think it's time
to be planning ahead

but knowing me
I'll settle for treading water
until my legs go numb
and the current drags me under

Rosemary Palmeira        IN THE VAPOUR BATHS

Cathedral of steam
soundproof chamber, where
only the heart breathes.

We strip off the outside world
step out of time and weather
and discordant voices;
lie naked on wooden boards
offered up to raining heat
swallowed up in vapour clouds.

Thoughts are slowly blotted out
blurred eyes are brought to focus
on a single point of light;
hardness starts to unloosen
as candle wax swills the taper,
heavy flesh translates to glaze,
the skin a sieve for moisture.
Heat and ice strafe the body
extinguish, ignite, transmute;
blood vessels strum, heart pumps fast;
all ugliness comes to surface -
washes away in pinprick showers.

I bring my broken body
my birth scars to the fierce heat
rigid bones slowly unclench
the breastplate across my chest melts.
Heat sprints up and down my limbs
I breathe and choke on scorched air;
tears fall onto this hot rain
relief seeps into each pore.
Extreme fatigue, jangling nerves
- all is absorbed and received;
I am accepted, renewed
I am utterly myself!

All violence and distortion
of chemistry and psyche
is contained here and assumed
into invincible fire.

Then
out into clear air
walk light as ether
a single eye, gleaming.

Dean Wilson    HAND OVER FIST

It was only December
and I could already taste the spring
so much so I brought it forward
and threw my hat into the ring

This is a downward spiral
Get out of the way
A spanner in the works is a good idea
when you're looking for an escape

It was just
one thing after another
Dodging cameras
Waiting 'round corners
Running errands
Taking orders
Smelling a rat
and carrying on regardless

So tell me
How much energy does it take
to get to where you want
when you don't know where it is?

All hands on deck
You'll never guess
how close I came
I am a martyr to the cause
of every man for himself
and mistress of all I survey

Lay the blame at my feet
and I'll take off my shoes and socks
Then walk backwards over Drypool Bridge
towards a garden that was once a dock

Ian Gregson     VENGEANCE IS MINE

The two were perfect friends,
Except they judged each other
Harshly over tidiness.
Only death would part them -
One was Catholic,
The other Anglican.

Sooner than they thought
They parted: from her window
The Anglican watches
Trying to imagine
What Hell means to her friend, this Hell
Lying about her age in her old age.

Since tidiness obsesses her
She must employ her walking-stick,
Eternally, to clear leaves
And litter from the street
Which grows fraught with meaning
Like a poem by God:

Its wicked never rest,
Its proud continually fall.
The author of her suffering
Shakes the autumn through downpours
At her hesitating feet;
The leaves are carried like lost souls
Forward and back in the wind.

Whose vengeance is this?

Sighs and lamentations
Swell from the railway-line,
The next circle; for the souls
Shrieking in the playground
Third childhoods last the longest -
Spinning and swinging
And jerking up and down.

Poor dear, she peers up
through her thick glasses
And can't remember where she is.

Nigel Walker      PILOT

The wheel turns by degrees.
Years pass. The moon has,
once again, pulled up the sea
to eider the emulsioned mud.
A chocolate river wrapped
in rainbow slicks
gives an exit from which
any coast is possible.
Rudders flick sideways, undecided.
Water breathes in; the North Sea
scratches icy fingers on the staith
and slaps the rusty metal
as it sighs and hesitates.
Years pass. Knowledge
of tow and depth, keeping afloat
become a thing not learned
but sensed. Nor can the stars,
pointing to north and east,
say which is best, which
windows will be broken, which
bricks cracked. The wheel turns.
We draw lines in pencil on a map;
the possibilities. Years pass.
An inch this way or that.

The difference
to our destination
could be huge.

Andrew Motion      SPURN

'Spurn Head?  That's a good place to be lonely'
Larkin was telling me, knowing my marriage
was on the rocks, his voice so easily over-
whelmed by the razzle-dazzle of the bar

I might be the one with dodgy ears, not him.
So he said it again, 'A good place to be lonely',
his eye lightening while he creamed a new pint,
and as it happened this time his words crashed

into one of those sudden, unexplained hushes
where a secret becomes a shout, and he saw
what he had done and was sorry, swivelling
away from the faces round us to look outside

instead at the empty walkways of the university,
and the summer wind bouncing between grey walls,
collecting, as it also happened, a silver crisp packet
and lifting it brilliantly up and over into sheer blue.

                            *

I bopped off alone next Sunday in my Renault,
alone and early, and the shit-canyon I lived in
brightened into the centre of Hull, then shrank
into the dry lanes of the Old Town (in those days

a forgotten elsewhere: yards of dead rope swaying
from lifting gear above the main cobbled street,
double-parked dredgers grinding heavily together
at the junction of the Hull and Humber, the hump-

backed bridge blistering in silence), then shot out
through east Hull with its bouncy-prison, its raw estates,
and the Holderness Road dead straight, dead flat,
then twirled round a white bump-in-the-road blob

which seemed nothing in particular to me but was in fact.
After that, it was not town any more but open country.
Not straight roads any more but side-stepping lanes.
Not feeling squeezed into myself any more, watching

everything I was and did, but cut loose from myself,
knowing where I was going but not how to get there.
The sun came out.  On my right I sensed the Humber
sometimes swelling towards me, sometimes away.

When I wound down my window, a holiday mud-smell
washed into the car and enveloped me, so that at once
I wanted to let myself laze and slip out of focus - except
the way wouldn't let me, no, just when I thought I had

a clear run, when my sails filled, a fence rose in front
so I slowed down or turned aside.  At one point I stopped
altogether and climbed a gate to take it all in.  Ripe wheat
as far as the horizon, and the breeze off the river stirring

watery crests and troughs.  Red-tiled farm-houses riding
gently at anchor, bobbing in the haze.  In a clump of elms -
this was before they all died - a rook-fleet all set one way.
After that, driving on again, with every breath the silence

sank deeper, the hedges thickened - scraping the sides
of the car sometimes, or smacking it with a bramble-hand -
and the wheat boiled up round the windows of a farm,
round the road-signs, round the drab evergreen glade

and the church where Andrew Marvell had been baptised,
or escaped through fence-poles and gate-ways to run riot
with cow-parsley and wormwood, fennel and campion,
with anything going on the narrowing road along me.

*

I stopped at Patrington church, which is another story,
although I can still hear the click forward and back of my heels
on its wet flagstones. Patrington. The Queen of Holderness.
On my way in, I peered up though holes carved in the spire

and each Gothic, mis-shapen, heart-shaped scrap of sky
seemed to be travelling faster than the rest of the world.
On my way out, the clock wheezed and struck mid-day,
so the notes wandered through the open door behind me

into the car. I took them to Easington, where the road
coiled back on itself, then straightened for the last stretch
and entered a different kind of flatness, everything
hunched and wind-whipped, Fields were smaller and cut,

their dark corduroy earth scored with scratches of sand.
Hedges were scrawny, worked tightly into each other.
There were no elms, only thorns with their arms flung up.
When I slowed at a junction, I realised the mood I was in

had changed from excited-careless to something like fear.
In front of me: I didn't know. Behind me, the whole country
I had gone through felt backed-up and bulky, ready to bear
down on me like a thunder-cloud in my rear-view mirror -

only there was no thunder-cloud, just sun. What Larkin
had said didn't explain it, and I wasn't thinking of marriage,
or not in detail, just admitting the shape of not-being
beside me in the car, and my disappointment.

*

What had begun as pleasure was no longer just pleasure.
I drove the last few miles as if I was going to judgement,
the name spiralling round and round inside my head.
I-don't-need-you-Point. Don't-come-near-me-Point. Spurn.

Everything about it said stay away, but I had seen it there
waiting on the map, dangling in the mouth of the Humber
from the north shore: a tongue, a comma, a thick eyelash,
a strip of skin; something which was neither earth nor water,

rock nor sand; bait for the enormous river-fish surging up
from Hull thirty miles to the west with every ebbing tide
and always taking the strike, losing a few boulders one time,
a rib of sand the next.  For centuries it had lived purely as itself,

slinking into the river, wanting to close it off, losing sand
from its seaward side, braiding it round the tip of the Point,
laying it along the river side.  Then the interference started.
Whalers setting out from Hull stripped its boulders for ballast

at the start of their journeys - and come the Atlantic fishing-
grounds, when they began filling their holds with whalemeat -
crashed them over the side in a fine litter across the ocean floor.
Every process leads to a crisis in time, of course.  This one meant

Spurn's sea-barricades grew threadbare, then were patched
with good intentions:  with groynes and walls and shingle dumps.
These worked, but they changed everything.  What had lived
by creeping slowly, by subterfuge, died when it just stood still.

*

The lane on the mainland lost confidence, then gave out
altogether.  I was on cement track now, with a sparse hackle
down the ridge.  A pill-box squinted at me from the sandbank.
A sentry-post rose up, and a barbed wire fence.  It was OK,

though, there were no soldiers - in fact there was nobody.
All this was just junk left over from the last war and useless,
which meant when I finally plucked up courage and stopped,
finally stopped, the silence seethed round me like boiling fat.

So I started walking, and half an hour later was still walking,
my head full of the effort of keeping going, everything else
part of that.  There was a high dune-wall running on my left,
sprinkled with clumps of marram and sea holly; on the right

a gradually widening pool - a slack backwater of the Humber,
coated with yellow scum, the sort of place you find dead dogs
and bits of herring-gull, and dolls, even when they're not there.
I put my head down and wouldn't look.  Halfway to the Point

there was the damage I had expected:  a hole in the dune-wall
and the cement track ripped up where the sea burst through.
It was a bomb-blast catastrophe - bewildering rips and tearings,
and weights too heavy for human lifting all flung about like balsa.

The wind, following where the sea had led, traced the shapes
over and over endlessly, making just-audible groans and whines,
and when I stared out through the dune-wall at the sea, blinding,
I saw the whole process of the years to come:  the waves crashing,

the track giving up the ghost entirely, the spindly Point cut off
and dawdling into the North Sea like someone who has forgotten
their name, and why they are here, and what the time is now,
and why anything matters, helpless and melting and then vanishing.

\*

At the first lighthouse, I was still between the dune-wall
and the expanding, idle backwater.  But with the Point almost
in view now, there was a feeling in me of things giving way -
as if the ground might be about to jink sideways under me

and I might step off into thin air.  Then came a second lighthouse,
with a cringing huddle of white cottages and a lifeboat station.
The boat itself looked like a scaled-down replica, perched
on a toy ramp which ran into the Humber.  But the river was real.

The river and the sea on my other hand which now floated
completely into vision as I took a few more steps, and the dune-
wall at last stumbled onto its knees.  I expected something
to come clear for me, but with the sun hurrying to and fro

between clouds, nothing could settle.  The waves charged in
and changed from grey to blue to green; at one moment
they were huge cascades; the next, skittering fragments.
The next nothing.  I understood that I could still turn back

but knew that I never would, and in a second or two
had taken myself to the crown of the Point, to the very tip,
where the wind blew so strongly my eyes ran and I leant
into it on trust.  On my left now, overwhelmingly close

and at the same time remote and not at all to do with me,
a rusty-nosed black container ship rode low in the water,
waiting for the tide to change so that it could come up-river.
The containers stacked on deck  were rusty bricks, immense

yet weightless.  The bridge was a tense eye where shapes
flitted and loomed.  In the waves around all this, smaller boats
sidled and surged: a hefty brown trawler, a red one, a green,
a white yacht for pleasure with its sails down and its engine on.

They were all poised to go, all fixed on the enormously wide
and open river, which seemed to be doing everything to stay calm
but was failing, tussling into little peaks and down into oily hollows.
Slap in front of me, where the ground I was standing on ran out

meekly underwater, the sea and the river met in a fault-line -
obstreperous breakers clashing then backing off, their children
quarrelling then making up, the whole brood swarming over
each other then leaving, then coming back for a last word.

\*

I sat down on the shore and watched this happen, half an eye
on the water, half looking in. Everything was fidgety and broken.
If I tried to think of marriage nothing came to me - no face, no voice,
no argument, nothing. When I thought of loneliness I had forgotten

how to feel it. I twisted round, shielding my eyes, and looked inland
along the river. I could see Immingham with its space-station refinery.
That must be the ferry over there, too far for me to make out
the mud-banks and derelict staves, the groyne taking its green strides

into oblivion. And that long ash-smudge - that must be Hull,
where I lived, and only this morning had set out from alone.
None of it had anything to do with me now. Not Hull, not anywhere. My existence was all here in sheer white sea-light

and smothering wind. Here between earth and water, rock
and sand, love and nothing. I climbed to my feet, shut my eyes,
felt the wind press its hand eagerly between my shoulder blades,
and began the journey back.

# Biographical Notes

**Carol Coiffait** lives and works in East Riding. A member of The Mutiny Writers and Subtle Flame, her poems have been published widely.

**Seamus Curran** was born in 1955 in Dundalk, Ireland. He came to Hull during the early 1980s, working as a builder and general labourer. At present he is on a BA English Literature course at Birbeck College in London.

**Peter Didsbury** moved to Hull at the age of six, and worked as an English teacher and subsequently as an archaeologist for Humberside County Council. He has published three widely-praised collections with Bloodaxe Books, most recently **That Old-Time Religion** (1994) which was a Poetry Book Society Recommendation.

**Helen Dunmore** was born in Beverley, Yorkshire, and is a writer for adults and children. Her latest poetry collection is **Bestiary** (Bloodaxe, 1997) and her new novel **Your blue-eyed Boy** has been published by Viking. She has won the Orange Prize for fiction and the Poetry Society's Alice Hunt Bartlett Award.

**Ian Gregson** was a postgraduate student at Hull University from 1974-77. Since then he has taught English at the University of Bangor, North Wales, and has become a prominent literary critic and reviewer.

**Douglas Houston** was at Hull University from 1966-69, and returned to the city during 1978-81. Both of his poetry volumes are from Bloodaxe: **With the Offal Eaters** (1986) and **The Hunters in the Snow** (1994). He now lives in West Wales and works as a freelance writer and researcher.

**Andrew Motion** was an English lecturer at Hull University from 1977-81. He has been the editor of **Poetry Review**, poetry editor for both Faber and Chatto & Windus, and is currently Professor of Creative Writing at the University of East Anglia. His publications include critical studies, best-selling biographies of **The Lamberts** (1986) and **Philip Larkin** (1993), and poetry collections, the latest being a **Selected Poems** (Faber, 1998).

**John Osborne** has taught American Studies at the University of Hull since the mid 1970s. Editor of the important literary magazine **Bête Noire**, he organised the complementary series of readings for over a decade, attracting large, enthusiastic audiences to various venues; events that successfully combined Hull-based talents with international writers.

**Rosemary Palmeira** was born in Portugal and now lives in Beverley. She is the author of **In the Gold of Flesh - Poems of Birth and Motherhood** (Women's Press, 1990). She has published poems and articles in various journals, and has performed her work.

**Ian Parks** was born in 1959. His association with Hull began in 1990 when he founded the Posterngate Writers Workshop, taught creative writing, and did a number of well attended readings. His first full-length collection of poems, **A Climb Through Altered Landscapes**, has just been brought out by Blackwater Press.

**Martin Peters** was born in York in 1968, studying photography in Harrogate and at Newcastle College of Arts. He is a professional photographer and a Visiting Lecturer at the University of Lincolnshire & Humberside. He has received several prestigious commissions and awards. Martin Peters can be contacted through the Association of Photographers.
Tel: (0171) 739 6669

**Shane Rhodes** was born in Hull in 1963. He is the editor of the international literary magazine **The Reater**, whose first issue appeared in 1997, and of Wrecking Ball Press. His poems have appeared in numerous magazines in the U.K. and U.S.A.

**Jules Smith** came to Hull as a student, and spent much of the 1980s completing a Ph.D on the Californian author Charles Bukowski. He was closely associated with John Osborne's **Bête Noire** magazine and reading series. His poems have appeared most notably in **The Faber Book of Movie Verse** (1993), his reviews in the **Times Literary Supplement**.

**Nigel Walker** was born in Liverpool in 1950. He now lives in Beverley, East Yorkshire, where he was a founder of Subtle Flame, an informal group for poets and musicians. His latest volume of poetry **Gold** appeared in 1996.

**Susan Wicks** studied French at Hull University, graduating in 1971. She is the author of three much-praised collections of poetry, two novels, and a short memoir, **Driving my Father**, all published by Faber.

**Dean Wilson** was born in Hull in 1965. Since 1988 he has worked in the City as a postman. He has given readings at various venues in Hull and London.

## Index of Images from the River Hull Corridor

*'Our feelings and mind maps of the places and people who inhabit our consciousness are complex and personally prompted by a thousand events that make up that priceless relationship of time and place called memory. When change takes place like some rude wind this at least must be protected.'*

Gerry Fitzhenry,
River Hull Corridor Project Director

Hull CityVision is the strategic focus for partnership working on urban regeneration.